"Herman, dinner's served... as soon as the smoke clears!"

HERMAN® by Jim Unger

Andrews, McMeel & Parker
A Universal Press Syndicate Company
Kansas City • New York

HERMAN® is syndicated internationally by Universal Press Syndicate.

"Herman, Dinner's Served . . . as Soon as the Smoke Clears!" copyright © 1985 by Universal Press Syndicate. All rights reserved. Printed in the United States of America. No part of this book may be used or reproduced in any manner whatsoever without written permission except in the case of reprints in the context of reviews. For information write Andrews, McMeel & Parker, a Universal Press Syndicate Company, 4400 Johnson Drive, Fairway, Kansas 66205.

ISBN: 0-8362-2068-4

Library of Congress Catalog Card Number: 85-61453

ATTENTION: SCHOOLS AND BUSINESSES

Andrews, McMeel & Parker books are available at quantity discounts with bulk purchase for educational, business, or sales promotional use. For information, please write to: Special Sales Department, Andrews, McMeel & Parker, 4400 Johnson Drive, Fairway, Kansas 66205.

"He's a bit nervous."

"So much for your theory that the earth is round."

5

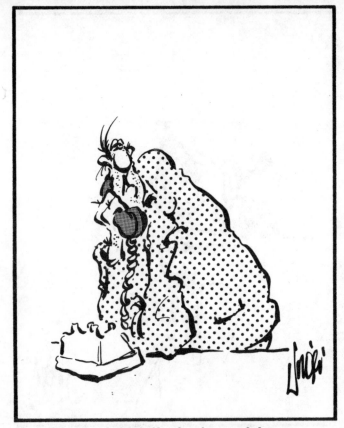

"It's me. I think I'm having a nightmare.
Check and see if I'm in bed."

"This'll take about 20 minutes."

"I've still got a few wrinkles to iron out."

"I still think these old statues are more comfortable than the modern stuff."

7

"We shot the decoy!"

"If you want to be a grandfather, you've got to make a few sacrifices."

"She hid all my clothes so I couldn't go
out tonight."

"What do you want on your hamburger?"

"The wife used to do quite a bit of modeling
. . . until she lost her tube of glue."

"OK. You can put your clothes back on."

10

"Your mother's been at my wine again."

"Salesman of the week gets to go to Hawaii."

"I never thought I'd see the day when I'd be out of work."

12

"Get your shoes off. I've just put down clean newspaper."

"He was only 35 years old when he did that one."

13

"Do you have any special plans for this pork chop?"

"I feel a lot better since I ran out of those pills you gave me."

15

"Have you got another menu? I can't afford anything on this one."

"Your previous employer says
you're unpredictable."

"You wouldn't believe the time we had
getting him down those stairs."

17

"If it looks like a close finish, jump off."

"Same to you!"

18

"I'm sure you've all been anxious to meet our
new company chairman."

"Run out the back and stick 'Happy Birthday'
on that for me."

19

"He'll be **42** years old next month."

"I'm sorry, sir, I just can't find it."

"Got any books about this wide?"

"Cheese omelet, sunny-side up."

"OK, five more minutes, then we'll go somewhere else."

"You'd better cancel the rest of my appointments."

22

"Catch of the day is the egg salad sandwich for $6."

"Chest, 68."

23

"Is there a band in front of me?"

"Couldn't you hear me knocking?"

24

"We didn't reserve a table. I brought
my own."

"You name it. I'm collecting for it."

"Two bedrooms."

26

"Did you see which way the camel went?"

"OK, here are your exam results."

27

"I can't listen to you *and* him at the same time."

"You can go back, Johnson, we got the door open."

28

"He's been driving me nuts since he did that dog food commercial."

"Anybody else like a cake?"

"I thought it was just one dog in the pet store."

"These clubs are going back to the store. They're useless."

30

"We've got 72 pictures of our wedding and he's not in one of them."

"Quick. Untie me, Maurice. Your mother's got my credit cards."

31

"That, my friend, is a
Tasmanian dive-bomber."

"OK. I'll be back to pick you up in 25 years.
What time?"

"The guy next door has gone away for the weekend. D'you wanna hear a singing telegram?"

"Let's go over to that new restaurant with the outside terrace and get some french fries."

33

"I told you not to open it."

"Is your daughter still in the same room?"

34

"This your idea, was it?"

"And you say your bike was chained to it."

"That's perfect, Wayne."

"Don't try to sneak by, sir."

36

"If you've stopped serving breakfast, I'll have a bowl of cornflakes for lunch."

"I bought you that tie 40 years ago and this is the first time you've worn it."

37

"Where's the top of my hot dog?"

"That too close?"

"Will you quit looking at your watch!"

"Rub this on everything within 50 feet of your house."

39

"We have two sorts of pies: undercooked and overcooked."

"I got a job as a night watchman in a mattress factory."

40

"You won't be able to write a check with your hands shaking like that."

"Fifteen years in the rat race, Ralph. Who needs it?"

41

"Don't tell me. Let me guess."

"Is your knee still bothering you?"

42

"Is the police cruiser still behind us?"

"I am *not* getting angry. I just want to know
what you mean by 'triplets.'"

43

"What do you mean, 'Put up the tent'?
That's it!"

"Where did you learn a word like that?"

"One day, kid, this will all be yours."

"You're not using enough gunpowder, Harry."

"Your horoscope says, 'Luck is on your side today. Don't be afraid to take risks.'"

"It's quite a friendly neighborhood."

46

"I'm out of horses until next Thursday."

"Is your mommy or daddy home?"

47

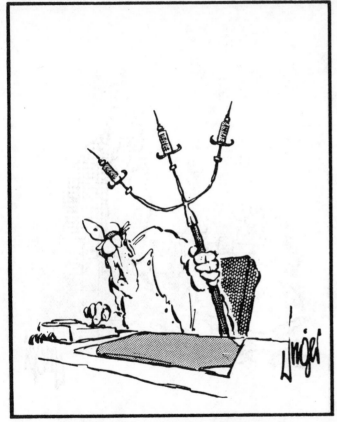

"Send in the next three patients."

"I told you not to call me at work after 9 o'clock."

"This is a good one! The guy's trying to make a date with the operator."

"I wanna try something. Grab both my legs and push."

"Sorry, pal. I just bought the planet. I want you and all your buddies off by next Friday."

"You must be the new sheriff."

"Where have you been all day? There's a mouse in the bedroom."

"Take a tip, pal. *Never* let them know you can read."

51

"It doesn't pay to advertise. Someone stole the dog."

"Do something, Dad! A big kid at school kicked me in the leg."

"What are you crying for? I promise you'll
have it back by tomorrow."

"I'm giving the goldfish a good swim."

53

"We'll have to eat in the kitchen. Your dinner's stuck to the stove."

"The baby-sitter fell asleep and some gangsters broke in and ate the rest of that chocolate cake."

"Today's topic is 'public awareness.'"

"Does car insurance cover ornamental fountains?"

"It's really stuck. Do you think you'll be able to play it like that?"

"They're keeping me in for observation."

"It's still wobbling."

"Now, now. . . . What's all this I hear about
you not wanting to come into my
nice hospital."

57

"Do you realize it's been 12 years since we went through the express checkout?"

58

"Do you *always* have to buy the cheapest cuts of meat?"

BEWARE OF THE DOG

BACK IN 5 MINS.

59

"OK, OK. *Not* guilty."

"What can I tell you?"

60

"It's our anniversary. What have you got that leaves a bad taste in the mouth?"

"OK, don't go crazy every time someone rings the front doorbell."

61

"You know you're on a diet. Why do you torture yourself?"

"Just how do you expect me to cook with these cheap saucepans?"

"Have you ever heard of the book 'How to Be Six Inches Taller'?"

"Do you mind slowing down?"

"I just cut hair. I don't book appointments."

"We ran out of poached salmon, so I gave you double potatoes."

64

"My guess is that it's doubled back on us."

"I lie awake nights wondering how you get a
10-speed bicycle down a chimney."

"Coffee for me, and he'll have a steak
sandwich. . . . Separate checks."

"Don't start looking for your glasses at
80 mph."

"Being discharged today! I just spent $8 on
these flowers."

"I can't sit in that waiting room all day,
doctor. I'm in a hurry."

67

"'Soup of the day' is the same as the 'soup of yesterday' with spaghetti in it."

"There we are. What's 350 pounds divided by two?"

"I put the kids to bed. I don't want them
watching stuff like this."

"Is this No. 11?"

"Anyone would think you're the only person in the world who was ever stung on the nose by a bee."

"Our first vice president."

70

"Say when."

"What happened to the picture?"

"You mustn't play with Grandpa's chair."

"Why did I have to be playing cards with the boys? For $500 a day, couldn't you be more creative?"

"What are my chances of time off for
good behavior?"

"Same old Christmas. He bought me a power
saw and I got him a pair of gold earrings."

73

"Mommy's not feeling too well, so I'm putting you in charge of cooking and cleaning."

"Can we get some service around here?"

"Just a minute, I can't find my keys."

"I gotta figure out a way to prevent it from falling over on its side when it stops rolling."

"Head office wants us to send someone to the Arctic."

"Why are you still wearing that cap? I've thrown it in the garbage three times."

76

"Let's face it, madame. Every swimsuit in this store is going to be a bikini for you."

77

"I get mixed up with Jupiter and Saturn. Why don't you ask at the gas station?"

"Five more minutes. Grandpa's been on his feet all day."

"I'll explain later. He had to go to the hospital."

"I guess you heard about the floods
on Mars?"

"Randolph, I'm talking to a real
live brontosaurus."

"Excuse me, sir, do you think I could trouble you to pass the salt?"

"If you must know, I don't like soap in my eyes."

80

"Muriel, he's gone."

"You expect me to tell the truth, the whole truth, and nothing but the truth, and then you ask me a question like that!"

"Watch out, Maurice. It may be a trap."

"He says there's definitely no intelligent life down here."

82

"When you read that letter of reference, you'll understand why I left."

"I don't think I've heard of you before, and I'm beginning to see why."

83

"Are you joking? Six dollars to send *that*?"

"I can't see Flipper or Goldie!"

"You said we could get a bigger car when the triplets were born."

"I'll let you decide, but they said the electricity will be off for at least an hour."

"I think he's gonna smash the TV if we don't let him out."

"We've been married 38 years and he says to me, 'How do you take your coffee?'"

86

"It's 3 o'clock in the morning."

"I told you not to go down there."

"She said she wants to look at some fur coats on Saturday, so I'm taking her to the zoo."

"I'm going to ask the warden if he'll let you look after Rusty for a couple of weeks."

88

"My pet snake swallowed a broom handle."

"You've got to be over at the park at 6 o'clock to fight Henry O'Grady's father."

"How do you say, 'We came to your country to find our suitcases'?"

"I'd like to borrow just enough to get myself out of debt."

"I need a door like this but with number 37 on it. . . . We're moving."

"I'll serve your dinner . . . as soon as the smoke clears."

"How's your back?"

"I can hear the ocean!"

"Couldn't you hear me shouting out there?"

"The plumber told you not to block
that overflow."

"Drop everything, Joyce. I want you to type this memo."

"Do we set our watches back 4,000 years or forward 4,000 years?"

"Come on . . . you won't get to be a guard dog just by looking at it."

"All the kids at your school sent you a get-well card."

"Did you see this? Three rooms of furniture for $15!"

"Only *you* would book a flight at 4:30 in the morning."

"I want you to start jogging three times a week. But not on Woodbine Crescent."

"Are you three all together?"

97

"I hope you don't expect me to pay for a three-minute lesson."

"Here, kitty, kitty."

"His hospital insurance runs out in 15 minutes."

"One . . . small . . . step for worms . . ."

"Why don't you write more clearly? You left a
$200 tip."

"If she agrees to cook, I think you could
spring for a color TV in the kitchen."

"I hope you realize you let your life insurance
run out in 1955."

"Would you like to donate something to the
charity of your choice?"

"Get down before you hurt yourself."

"How can a 2-ounce chocolate bar add on 4 pounds?"

"Your last five dates all went back to their ex-husbands."

"Maurice, he got it home and it was too tight across the shoulders."

"I forgot their crummy password again."

"I doubt if you'd know it. It's a very small country."